# Contents

Thanks to Brian Mackinney for compiling the text. Reviewed for the second edition by Alan Fergus. Photographs of the rounders ball on page 7 and the back cover by Mike Ellis. Photographs on front cover, back cover, inside front cover, inside back cover and pages 8, 12, 15, 17, 22, 24, 27, 29, 34, 38 and 43 by MC Photography courtesy of the NRA. All other photographs by Chris Libina of Sporting Pictures (UK) Ltd.

*Note* Throughout the book players and umpires are referred to individually as 'he'. This should, of course, be taken to mean 'he or she' where appropriate. All measurements are in metric units.

# Foreword

On behalf of the National Rounders Association, I am delighted to say that *Know The Game Rounders* has proved to be a popular publication. It provides a sound basis on which to build rounders skills and an understanding of the game.

Rounders is going from strength to strength. From primary school to adult level, the game is being played more competitively than ever before, and coaching and umpiring at all levels has become more structured. Along with the introduction of the National Rounders Association Rules these developments have helped to raise the standard and pace of the game to an exciting level.

**Shirley Walker**
**Chairman**
**National Rounders Association**

# Introduction

- Rounders is played by both children (especially at school) and adults.
- Being a non-contact sport, rounders is especially suitable for mixed-gender and mixed-age teams.
- The rounders player develops batting, bowling and fielding skills.
- Rounders teams are usually made up of families and friends.
- At first, teams play friendly matches against other groups.
- Only three teams are needed to form a league.
- Assistance can be obtained from the National Rounders Association.

# The National Rounders Association

The National Rounders Association (NRA) was formed in 1943 and is now responsible for and has the copyright of the rules of the game – the national rules.

The NRA encourages prospective umpires and coaches to take tests in order to maintain the standard of the game.

The NRA is supported by Sport England and by the Foundation for Sport and the Arts, and in turn provides support for all those interested in rounders – from the beginner to the international player.

By affiliating to the NRA, it is possible to keep abreast of the changes and developments in the game as they occur. Application forms are available from the NRA Affiliations Secretary at the following address. All correspondence should be sent to the NRA National Office: 55 Westlands Gardens,Westfield,Sheffield,S20 8ES. (Tel: 0114 2480357).

The NRA official web site can be found at http://rounders.punters.co.uk

## Tournaments

Details of NRA tournaments are available from the NRA Tournament Secretary at the address given above.

## Awards Scheme

Details of the NRA Awards Scheme are available from the NRA Schools Secretary at the address given above.

# The game

Rounders is played by two teams, ideally with a maximum of nine players on each side. A game may, however, proceed with as few as six players on either team. In a mixed team, a maximum of five males should be permitted. Six named substitutes per team are allowed. Each team bats in turn while the other fields, a full game allowing for each team to have two innings.

The object of the batting team is to hit the ball in such a direction and to such a distance that the batter can run round four posts before the next ball is bowled and score a 'rounder'. If the batter hits the ball and reaches second post then a half rounder is scored (unless the batter is put out before another ball has been bowled). If the batter fails to hit, but still runs round the four posts, a 'half rounder' is scored. A half-rounder is also awarded if two consecutive 'no-balls' are bowled to one batter, and as a penalty for obstruction by a fielder. The team scoring the most rounders wins.

The batter can stay at any post on the way round, reaching fourth post several balls later. He then has another hit in his turn.

The bowler and fielders work together to get the batters out as quickly as possible, and to prevent them scoring.

The bowler stands in the bowling square and the backstop stands behind the batting square so that he does not obstruct the hitting action of the batter.

Most teams have one fielder on first post. The rest of the fielders are arranged according to the age and ability of the players.

The rules govern the way the ball is bowled and also the position of the batter and the direction in which he hits the ball. Other rules are designed to prevent obstruction, etc., so that the game can be very exciting if played by skilled players working together as a team.

The NRA publication *The Official Rules and Hints to Umpires* is available from the NRA Publications Secretary at the address given on page 3.

## Substitutes

Six substitutes, nominated prior to the start of the game, may join in at any dead ball situation after first informing the umpires and the other team. In a mixed team, a maximum of five males per team may be on the field of play at any one time.

## Innings

A full game consists of two innings, and the team with the greater number of rounders shall win the game.

A team leading by five or more rounders at the completion of the first innings shall require the team with the lower score to bat again. Should the team with the lower first innings score be unable to better its opponents' score, then the game shall be declared over.

# Equipment

The equipment which is required to play rounders is simple and inexpensive to buy. All equipment should be manufactured for the purpose, and be approved by the NRA. Details of the equipment safety policy can be obtained from the NRA Equipment Secretary at the address given on page 3.

## The bat

Each member of the batting team should have a rounders bat. As the batter has to carry the bat around the track, the minimum number of bats per team should be five.

The bat can be of any length up to a maximum of 46 cm. It should measure not more than 17 cm round the thickest part and weigh no more than 370 g. Bats are made of wood, aluminium or plastic. Of the wooden type, one with a spliced handle bound with string is the most economical. A bat which is made all in one piece and with an unbound handle may not stand up to constant wear, especially as hitting improves.

# The ball

A rounders ball should be made of leather, weigh between 65 and 85 g, and measure a minimum of 18 cm and a maximum of 20 cm in circumference. Its core is similar to that of a cricket ball, and the best quality are covered in white kid.

It is advisable to use cheaper balls for practice, and specially made hard-wearing balls when playing on asphalt. They are all the same size and weight as the standard ball.

Only NRA licensed balls should be used in matches.

# The posts

Four posts are used, each 1.2 m high, with a heavy base so that they are not knocked over easily, or blown over by the wind. The base should have no sharp projections or points, and the collar (where applicable) in which the post is fitted should be no higher than 50 mm.

For the purposes of the rules, the base supports the post and the latter should be touched with the ball by the fielder. If the base and post are separated, then the base should be touched. If the base is moved from the marked spot, then the spot should be touched.

Posts driven into the ground are not permitted. The NRA recommends the use of rubber bases.

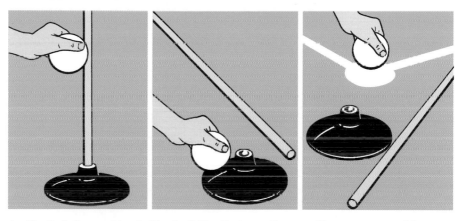

▲ *Fig. 1 Left – post touched by the fielder. Centre – if post and base are separated, base must be touched. Right – if base has moved from the marked spot, spot must be touched.*

# Clothing

Normal games clothing and footwear is worn for rounders.

Where teams play in similar uniform, they can be identified by coloured bands, arms bands or playing bibs. During a match, all players – substitutes included – must be clearly numbered.

Spiked footwear is prohibited, including cricket boots. Studs are allowed providing they are no longer than 12 mm.

# The pitch

## The playing area

Any surface on which it is possible to run quickly (e.g. Asphalt, gravel or grass) is suitable. Mixed surfaces are not recommended.

The area required is about the size of a soccer pitch. A large area makes for a more open game, and both fielding and hitting improve. An enjoyable game can be played on a smaller area, even one surrounded by walls.

Avoid marking the pitch in the corner of the playing area as this restricts hitting. The forward/backward line should be parallel to the boundary fence.

Whatever the size of the playing area, certain distances must be standard. The essential measurements are:

* the bowling and batting squares, because bowler and batter must get used to their restricted movement

* the distance between batting and bowling squares, so that the bowler can maintain his length
* the distance between the batting square and first post, because of the importance of the backstop's throw to first post.

Other distances can be less accurate without spoiling the game.

The simplest way of marking the positions of the posts relative to the batting square is by using lengths of string. Put a peg into the ground where the right hand front corner of the batting square is to be, and directly opposite that, another peg at a distance of 17 m. This gives the position of second post. Take a length of string measuring 24 m and tie a knot in the centre (each half 12 m). Tie one end of the string to each peg and carry the centre knot out to the right until the string is taut. The knot gives the position of first post; mark it with a peg.

Carry the centre knot to the left. Pull the string taut. The knot gives the position of third post; mark it with a peg.

Take a length of string, 17 m long with a centre knot (each half 8.5 m), and tie one end to the peg at third post and the other to the peg first put in at the corner of the batting square. Carry the string to the left until it is taut. The knot gives the position of fourth post; mark it with a peg.

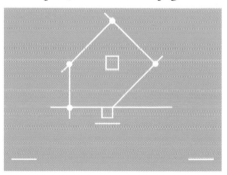

▲ *Fig. 2  The pitch: compulsory markings*

9

## The bowling square
## (2.5 m x 2.5 m)

To locate the centre of the front line of the square, stretch the 17 m string from the first peg to the second post, then measure a distance of 7.5 m along the string. The front line of the bowling square will then be 1.25 m either side of the string and parallel to the front line of the batting square. The other three sides of the square can then be marked. It will be found that if the string is stretched between the first and third posts, it cuts the side lines of the square 1 m from the front line.

## The batting square
## (2 m x 2 m)

The front line is made by marking a line extending 2 m from the first peg towards, and in a direct line with, fourth post, and parallel to the front line of the bowling square. The remaining three sides of the square can then be marked. The front line of the square should be extended on each side. This will separate the backward and forward areas. A line should also be marked from the front right-hand corner of the batting square to the first post position.

At least 10 m behind the back-ward/forward area line, and 15 m either side of the front right-hand corner of the batting square, lines will be drawn to mark the positions for waiting batters and batters out.

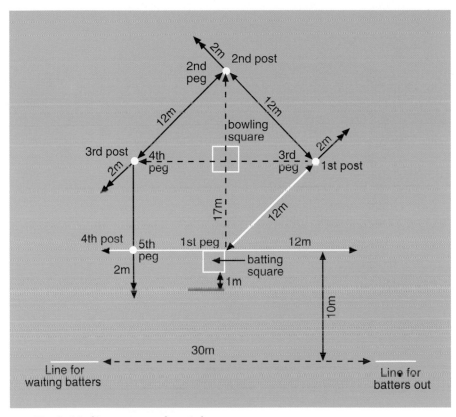

▲  *Fig. 3   Marking out a rounders pitch*

11

# Basic rules

The rules of rounders have become more detailed as the game has developed. If you play in a competitive league or tournament it is suggested that you play to the national rules. When you first play the game it is possible to play to basic rules, as long as everybody plays to the same rules.

## Teams

- Teams consist of a maximum of nine players and a minimum of six.
- Mixed teams should have a maximum of five males.

## Scoring

- A rounder is scored if, after hitting the ball, the batter runs round the track and touches fourth post.
- A half rounder is scored if, after hitting the ball the batter reaches second post and is not out before another ball is bowled.
- A half rounder is scored if, after missing the ball, the batter runs round the track and touches the fourth post.
- A half rounder is scored if the fielder, in the opinion of the umpire, obstructs the batter.
- A half rounder is awarded to the fielding team if a batter, while waiting to bat, obstructs a fielder.

## Bowling

The bowler should deliver the ball:

- with a smooth and continuous underarm action
- with both feet within the bowling square before the ball is released
- within the reach of and to the hitting side of the batter
- below the top of the batter's head or above his knee
- so that it is not bowled directly at the batter
- so that it does not bounce before reaching the batting square.

By failing to comply with any of the above, the bowler will be deemed to have bowled a no-ball.

## Batter out

A batter is declared out if:

- the ball is caught from the bat or the hand holding the bat (except on a no-ball)
- his foot projects over the front or back line of the batting square during the hitting action (except on a no-ball)
- he runs inside a post unless forced to do so by an obstructing fielder
- a fielder touches a post to which a batter is running, with the ball or with the hand holding the ball
- he obstructs a fielder or intentionally deflects the ball
- he overtakes another batter
- he loses contact with a post while waiting at it, if the bowler has possession of the ball in the bowling square
- he leaves a post at which he is waiting during the bowler's action, but before the ball is released
- he deliberately drops or throws the bat.

# Starting the game

A coin is tossed by the captains for choice of innings, and the winner decides either to field or to bat.

Fielding positions vary depending on the proficiency of the players, but the team needs to have a bowler, a backstop and a first post fielder.

The fielding team will take up their accustomed fielding positions – those places where they themselves hit and where they might also expect their opponents to hit. The captain should change the fielding positions when the capabilities of the batters have been assessed. The fielding positions may need to change if a left-hander is batting.

The batting side must wait in the backward area behind the marked lines. If a waiting player moves from these lines and impedes a fielder, a half rounder is awarded to the fielding team. The batting side should use the waiting time to study the bowling and the placing of the fielders, and to judge the other team's capabilities.

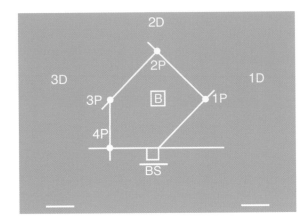

▲ *Fig. 4 Standard fielding positions: arrange the field to suit the ability of the players. Key: B – bowler; BS – backstop; 1P – first post; 2P – second post; 3P – third post; 4P – fourth post; 1D – first deep; 2D – second deep; 3D – third deep, etc.*

14

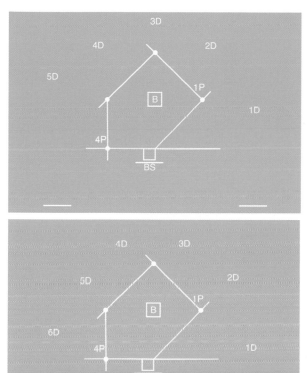

◀ *Fig. 5  Fielding positions:*
*five deep fielders; backstop*
*covering fourth post*

◀ *Fig. 6  Fielding positions:*
*six deep fielders; bowler taking*
*fourth post with backstop*
*covering; backstop taking*
*fourth with first post fielder*
*covering*

# The eyes have it

Whether you are batting, bowling or
fielding, the eyes have it.

# Batting

## In the batting square

A batter should:

• walk, and not run, to the batting square when called by the batter's umpire
• concentrate on the game, all the time
• watch the bowler – he may move about in his square in an unfamiliar way.

The batter can stand where he likes in the square, so long as his feet do not cross the front or back line while he is hitting or trying to hit the ball. If he is slow on his feet he may find it better to stand as near as he can to the first post.

Before hitting the ball, the batter should study the position of the fielding team and then try to place the ball into the least protected position in the forward area. A ball placed well in the deep, over the head of the first post fielder, is further from fourth post; this is a hit which does not come naturally to right-handed players and must be practised.

## How to hit

Stand sideways to the bowler when receiving the ball, i.e. right-handed players have the left shoulder forwards and their weight on the left foot. Watch the ball from the bowler's hand all the way onto the bat. Hold the bat so that the tip is above the level of the wrist.

Some players hold the bat in front of them, letting the weight of the bat be taken by the other hand. Others find it helpful to prepare for the hit by holding the bat behind them in the backlift position. At the right moment the bat is swung forwards to meet the ball.

In batting there are four important points to master.

• **Arm movement**. The arm should be swung back from the shoulder with the elbow lifted away from the body; it should not be a stiff action. The ball is hit by quickly straightening the elbow with a strong swift flick and a turn of the hand so that the knuckles are facing the ground. This turn of the wrist and arm adds speed to the hit and direction to the ball. More proficient players will find that the quick backward swing of the bat also adds power to the stroke.

● **Footwork.** As the ball approaches, the batter has a split second to decide how he will move his feet in order to make the hit. If he is right-handed and holds his bat lifted, his weight should be on the right foot. As he swings the bat forwards his weight is transferred to the left foot. If the bat is held out in front, the weight is swung on to the right foot as the bat is raised backwards, then forwards on to the left foot as the hit is made; this will give more power to the stroke. The batter need not stand still in the square; the space is his to use.

● **Turning the shoulders.** If the shoulders are turned as the hit is made, it adds force to the stroke.

● **Timing.** The arm, foot and shoulder movements must be blended into one continuous action. Only practice will help the player to lift the arm just before the ball reaches him, so that he can swing forwards to hit as he changes his weight and turns his shoulders. A well-timed hit, with a good follow through, is very exhilarating. A batter should learn to 'dance' in the square, with weight evenly balanced. As he hits, he should step forwards on to his left foot, turn his shoulders, flick the wrist and flash the ball away.

## Running a rounder

Each batter is entitled to one 'good' ball and having hit, or attempted to hit it, he must leave the batting square and run round the track. If he reaches and touches fourth post before the next ball is bowled, he scores one rounder if he hit the ball, or a half-rounder if he missed it (he is deemed to have hit the ball if he struck it with the bat, or with the hand holding the bat).

He may stay at any post on his way round, where he is safe providing he keeps contact with the post with his hand or bat. When further balls are bowled he may run on to the next post or further, but when he reaches fourth post he cannot score. Once round, he remains in the backward area until it is his turn to bat again. When batters are out, the sequence of the batting order remains unchanged.

## Points to remember

● Touching a post – puts out a batter who is moving towards it from the previous post.
● Touching a post – prevents the 'live' batter (the one to whom the current ball was bowled) from scoring if he is within reach of the previous post. For instance: if the 'live' batter has reached first post, second post should be touched; if he has reached second post, third post should be touched; if he has reached third post, fourth post should be touched.
● Touching a post – has no other effect on the game and does not prevent any batter from running right round the track, including running to posts which have been touched.
● The ball is in play from the time it leaves the bowler's hand until he again has possession of the ball and is in the square.
● A batter may continue his run round the track unless the bowler has the ball and is in his square. There is no other way of stopping him.

In fig. 7, stumping fourth post puts out batter A. It does not prevent the other batters from getting home safely, nor does it prevent batter D from scoring.

Stumping second post would prevent batter D from scoring but again would not prevent any batter running to fourth post on this ball.

On the way round the track the batter may stop at a post if the fielding is better than he expected and it seems dangerous to go on. Should the fielders misjudge a throw, the batter will run on again. If he succeeds in reaching fourth post, a rounder is scored.

For example, a batter hits a ball well into the deep and runs. He reaches second post and makes contact with the post, thinking he cannot get to fourth post. The deep fielder overthrows the ball – he meant it for the bowler, and it pitches just outside first post. The batter sees he can safety run on, and arrives at fourth post, scoring a rounder.

If, on the other hand, the batter has to stop and a fielder touches the post immediately ahead of the one of which he is within reach, the batter can run on but he cannot score.

For example, a batter has reached third post. A fielder touches fourth post and then throws the ball carelessly back to the bowler who misses it. Nobody is backing up so the ball trickles away between second and first posts. The batter gets home with ease, but because the post immediately ahead was touched while he was trying to score a rounder, he does not score. The umpire calls 'no score'.

- A batter should always run as far as he can in order to clear the way for the next batter who may be a good runner.
- There can never be two batters at one post. For example, a batter is at second post and he is caught up by the next batter. The umpire orders the first batter to run on and he may then be put out at third post.
- A batter is out if he runs inside a post.

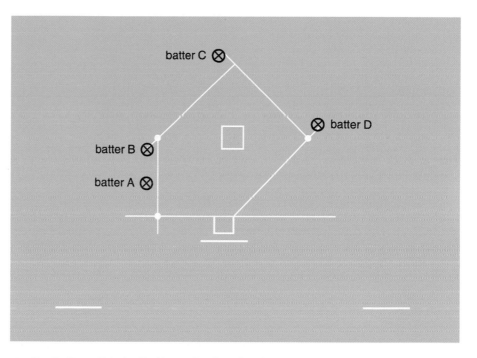

▲ *Fig. 7   Batter D is the 'live' batter. Touching fourth post puts out A, but does not prevent D from scoring*

# Keeping contact with the post

When a batter is at a post he should either hold it with his hand or keep in contact with it with his bat. If he loses contact he can be put out by any fielder who touches the next post with the ball in hand.

The best way for the batter to keep in contact with the post is for him to change his bat to his left hand as he runs, and then be ready to go on to the next post. He can move on as soon as the next ball leaves the bowler's hand. If a batter overruns the post, he may come back and make contact with that post, providing he has run straight on and has not altered his direction. To stay in, the batter must have touched the post before the fielder.

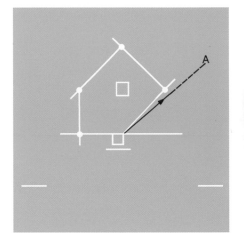

▲ *Fig. 8  If the batter is running so quickly that he overruns the post (A), he is allowed to return to the post. If he runs on in the direction of the next post, he may not return*

## Obstruction by a batter

A batter should run from post to post in a direct line. If he does so, he is in no danger of obstructing a fielder and has right of way. If he runs off his direct course and in so doing collides with a fielder and prevents him from fielding, he will have caused an obstruction and will be given 'out' by the umpire. Any rounder scored due to that obstruction will be declared void.

A batter is out if he deliberately kicks or touches the ball as he runs round the track. The running track extends 2 m beyond fourth post.

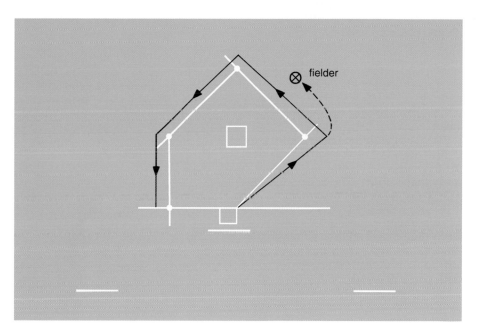

▲ *Fig. 9 If the batter runs off course (dotted line) and obstructs a fielder, he is out*

# No-balls

The ball must be bowled so that is would reach the batter within the limits shown in fig. 10 below.

- AB – level with the top of the batter's head.
- CD – level with the batter's knees.
- AD – the limit of the batter's reach.
- BC – a line by the side of the batter's body (balls close to the body and difficult to hit are not no-balls).

This imaginary rectangle will vary according to the stature and reach of each batter, and will be on the opposite side for left-handed players.

If the ball would not pass within these limits, the umpire will call 'no-ball' and the batter then need not run. If he does so he may score in the usual way. He cannot be caught out from a no-ball, or touched out at first post, nor can he be given 'out' for a foot over the front or back line. If, therefore, a player finds that no-balls which are too high or too low are easy to hit, he should go all out for them, as he knows he cannot be caught out.

Umpires will not call 'no-ball' if the batter turns good balls into no-balls by walking into them or by stepping away to make them wide. Some players, finding hitting difficult, unconsciously make one of these mistakes.

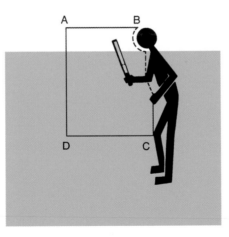

▲ *Fig. 10  Judging a no-ball: the imaginary rectangle*

# A backward hit

Fig. 11 shows the backward area. If the batter mistimes his shoulder turn or moves his feet too soon, the ball may drop into this area. If this happens the batter is only allowed to run to the first post. He may, however, run on immediately the ball crosses the forward/backward line. This may be during its flight from the fielder who retrieves it, and the moment it passes this line the batter may run on again. If the fielding is slow he may reach fourth post and score a rounder.

A ball that strikes the ground in the forward area and which then rolls or bounces into the backward area is not a backward hit.

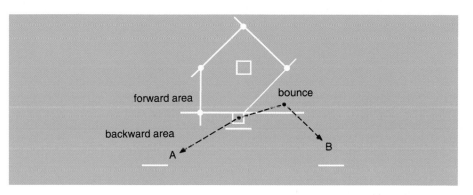

▲ *Fig. 11 A is a backward hit. But if the ball touches the ground in the forward area and then goes in the backward area (B), it is not a backward hit*

▼ *Fig. 12 Forward or backward hit?*

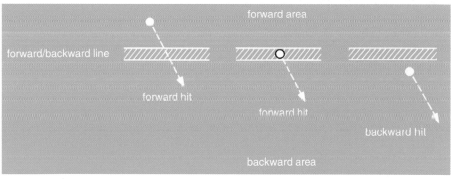

# Batter out

A batter shall be declared out:

- if the ball is caught from the bat or the hand holding the bat except on a no-ball
- if his foot projects over the front or back line of the batting square before he hits the ball or it has passed him, except on a no-ball
- if he runs to the inside of a post, unless prevented from reaching it by an obstructing fielder
- if a fielder touches the post immediatly ahead with the ball or the hand holding the ball while the batter is running to that post and before the batter has touched the post, except first post in the case of a no-ball
- if he obstructs or verbally misleads a fielder, or intentionally deflects the course of the ball
- if he overtakes another batter
- if he loses contact with a post or runs at any time when the bowler has the ball and is in his square (except on an overrun or unless ordered to do so by an umpire)
- if he loses contact with a post or runs during the bowler's action before he releases the ball
- if, after having been ordered to make contact with a post, he has not done so
- if he drops or throws his bat deliberately.

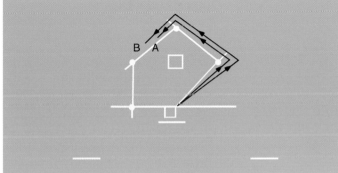

▲ Fig. 13  Batter B is out for overtaking A

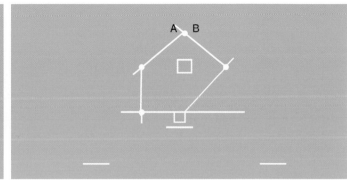

▲ Fig. 15  Two batters at a post. A has to run on. If the next post is touched while he is running to it, he is out

▼ Fig. 14  Batter A is out for running inside the post

▼ Fig. 16  If second post is touched before Batter A arrives, A is out. Batter B can stay at the post

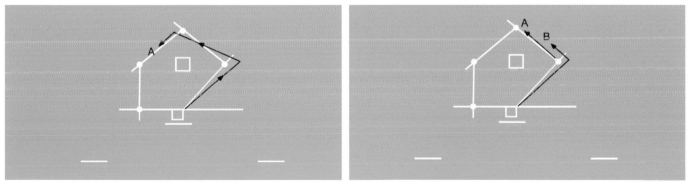

## Side out

Where there is no batter awaiting his turn to bat, all the batters on the running track can be put out simultaneously by the ball being thrown full pitch or touched into the batting square by any fielder, before any of the batters have reached and touched fourth post.

Where there is no batter waiting his turn to bat, and the bowler has possession of the ball in the bowling square so that no batter can leave a post, the side shall be declared out.

▲ *Fig. 18   Side out: the ball is touched into the square*

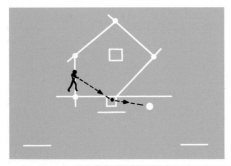

▲ *Fig. 17   Side out: the ball is thrown full pitch into the batting square*

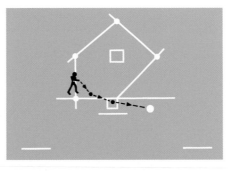

▲ *Fig. 19   Not out: if the ball pitches outside the square and then travels into the square, the batter is not out*

## Last player in

If only one batter is left, he is given the choice of three 'good' balls. He need not run when the first two 'good' balls are bowled, but when he receives the third 'good' ball he must run, and the fielding side must try to put him out in any normal way or place. As usual, touching fourth post will have no effect unless he has passed third post.

Should he fail to hit all three balls, the backstop puts him out by placing the ball in the batting square and the innings is closed. The last batter can score from any no-balls which he receives. He cannot be caught off a no-ball, but if he runs he can be put out in the normal way. If he scores a rounder, he is entitled to a rest of one minute, and then has the choice of three more 'good' balls and so on *ad infinitum*.

# Bowling

The bowling action is based entirely on underarm throwing. The simplest method for a beginner to practise is an underarm throw aimed at the backstop's hands.

## Action

Stand sideways to the backstop with the weight on the right foot. Change the weight to the left foot as the arm swings. As the ball leaves the hand, turn the shoulders with a strong follow through towards the batter.

When learning to bowl, try to visualise the rectangular space into which your ball must go.

A no-ball will be called if:

• the ball, when it reaches the batter is outside the limits of the imaginary rectangle described on page 22
• the ball fails to reach the batter

• the bowler steps out of the bowling square during the bowling action, i.e. before releasing the ball
• the ball bounces before reaching the batter.

The ball must be bowled in the direction of the batting square. A player losing contact with a post through a dummy ball will be allowed to return to his original position.

# Footwork

When the simple bowling action has been learnt, bowlers will find that they can make the ball travel faster if they step forward as they bowl.

Stand at the back of the bowling square with your left side towards the batter. Hold the ball in the right hand and point the left arm in the direction in which you are bowling.

Step sideways with the left foot, lift your right arm behind you and close the right foot up to the left.

Now step forwards with the left foot, bend the left knee, turn the shoulders and bowl.

While swinging the right arm forwards, balance the body by simultaneously swinging the left arm backwards. This action should be smooth and rhymical.

# Suggestions

From the simple bowling action other ideas can be practised.

## Speed

• The length of the bowling square (2.5 m) allows for a run up before the ball is released. The bowler can step out of the square once the ball has been released. This allows for the bowler to increase his momentum and therefore the speed at which the ball can be delivered.
• Learn to change the speed of delivery with the same bowling action.

## Spin and swing

• Change the grip, and by turning the fingers as the ball is released the ball will spin.
• Change the grip and change the swing of the arm, then the ball will swing either away from or into the batter.

▲ *Fig. 20   The bowler can step out of the square once the ball is released*

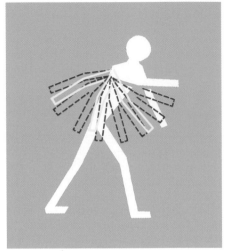

▲ *Fig. 21   Use the same action, but change the delivery to deceive the batter*

# Direction

- Change the angle of the run across the square and the ball will arrive at the batter from a different direction.
- Lower the position of the hand on delivery and the ball will rise up at the batter.
- A 'donkey-drop' – a high ball which arrives at the batter at the correct height – falls down towards the batter.

## Different hands

If the bowler can bowl equally well with either hand, he should do so.

*Note* All bowling variations should be delivered with a smooth and continuous underarm action, and produce a 'good' ball as defined by the rules.

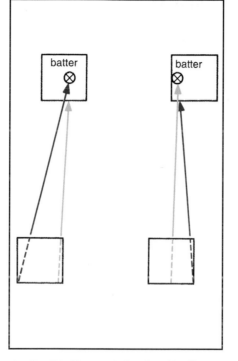

▲ *Fig. 22 Change of direction: blue line – bowler runs straight across the square; red line – bowler runs diagonally across the square*

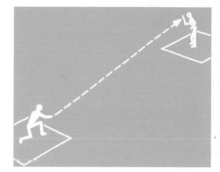

▲ *Fig. 23 By bending the knees in the running stride, the bowler can release the ball lower than normal so that it rises up at the batter*

▼ *Fig. 24 The donkey-drop: a high ball which reaches the batter at the correct height*

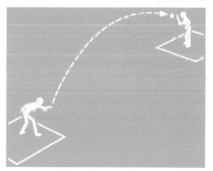

31

# Fielding

## Fielding as a team

Fielding is a team game. Each fielder should be on the alert through the innings.

Fielders should be ready to move, not rooted to the spot. If they have their eye on the ball they will always be ready to back up and cover other fielders.

In a game for beginners, the fielders are arranged in two semi-circles. The inner semi-circle contains the four post fielders and the backstop. The outer semi-circle consists of the three deep fielders who cover the post fielders and field long hits. The ninth player is the bowler.

Field placings can change throughout an innings. Fielders should watch for directions from the backstop, who is in the best position to see the whole field. The bowler and backstop should be aware of strong or weak batters, and left-handers.

The very best teams change the composition of the semi-circle system. The inner semi-circle comprises the bowler, backstop and first post fielder. The backstop covers fourth post. The outer semi-circle contains the other six fielders in an arc. All the fielders are ready to cover each other.

The fielding team arranges the field placings to keep the opponents' scoring to a minimum.

If a batter makes a hit, touching the post ahead of the post he has reached prevents the rounder from being scored. Returning the ball to the bowler, in the bowling square, before the 'live' batter reaches the third post also prevents the rounder from being scored.

## Look out!

• The area behind first post is very vulnerable. The first deep fielder has to be especially aware all the time. Few hits go there, but when they do they can be winning ones

• Have a plan of action for when a batter hits the ball. Each fielder should know what to do and where to throw the ball. This saves thinking time, and makes fielding smoother and more efficient.

• Do not chase a 'live' batter round the posts by throwing the ball from post to post. Panic sets in and the batter usually wins.

• Beware of obstructing a running batter, especially in the vicinity of the posts. The first post fielder should be careful when receiving bad throws from the backstop which could force an obstruction. The first post fielder can catch the ball and allow the batter to reach the post or leave the ball for the first deep fielder to field. The ball can then be returned to the bowler. Remember, a batter who is obstructed, in the opinion of the umpire, is awarded a half rounder.

• Make all throws to the bowler and the fielders at the posts accurate so that they can do their jobs efficiently.

• Remember, more than one batter can be put out at a time. Fielders should be aware of all the opportunities.

# Catching

It is very important to get into the correct position for catching. More catches are missed by failure to do this than by failure of the hands to close on the ball.

The aim of the catcher can be summarised as follows.

• He should move quickly to get in line with the flight of the ball.
• When in this position, the body should be kept balanced and the ball should be watched closely.
• The aim should be to catch the ball level with the face.
• The fingers should be spread so that the ball is caught in the web so formed.
• The hands should 'give' to the force of the ball. This 'give' is generally in the direction in which the ball is already travelling, though sometimes a ball can be snatched out of its path. More 'give' is needed to retain a fast-travelling ball than a slow one.

If a ball is going over the catcher's head he should move back quickly, keeping his weight forwards. If it is a very long hit, he should turn round and run hard so that he may at least be able to field it on its first bounce, even if he fails to catch it. Short quick steps are best if a fielder has to move to the left or right to get behind wide balls. Two hands are naturally safer than one in all catching, but right- and left-hand catching should be practised.

# Fielding balls on the ground

A ball travelling along the ground must be gathered as quickly as possible. Practise fielding this kind of ball approaching from both the right and the left.

Fielders must be mobile and must keep their eyes on the action of the bowler and batter. They will be quicker off the mark if they stand with their weight distributed equally on both feet. As the ball is hit they should change the weight to the balls of the feet, slightly bend their knees, keep their arms and hands ready, and start moving into the line of the ball.

Fielders should try to anticipate the ball's line of flight. If it is moving slowly, they should run to meet it. If it is moving quickly, they should run to get behind it. Fielders should always be able to see their hands as they pick up the ball. The wrists should be forwards and the hand should go round the ball. The ball should be moved quickly into the throwing hand and returned, so that the fielding is speeded up.

When stopping the ball the fielder should get right behind it and watch it right into the hands. Most fields are uneven and the ball can bounce awkwardly and unexpectedly. The 'gate' fielding position allows for more of the body to cover the ball in order to stop it if it bounces away from the hands.

# Throwing

## Overarm throwing

The ball is thrown above or about the level of the shoulders. This throw is used for long distances and needs plenty of practice to make sure of accuracy.

### Action

Stand sideways to the player to whom the ball is to be thrown, with the weight on the back foot (ie. The right foot if the ball is held in the right hand).

Bend the throwing arm slightly and hold it well away from the body. Drop the shoulder of the throwing arm and raise the other arm to give balance. Now bring the front shoulder and arm into the line of direction of the throw.

Make the throw by a strong forward turn of the shoulders, bringing the hand with the ball forwards by extending the elbow and flexing the wrist. Complete the throw by transferring the weight on to the front foot and bring the throwing shoulder into the lead. This simultaneous change of weight and twist of the shoulders gives ease of movement and adds length to the throw. A strong wrist flick helps the flight of the ball.

The ball must be thrown directly into the hands of the fielder who is receiving the ball, for three reasons:

- a bounced ball is often difficult to catch because the surface of the ground is seldom flat
- as the post area is small and crowded with players, a post fielder may have difficulty in fielding a ball unless it falls directly into his hands. There is always the added danger that he may obstruct a batter
- a direct throw is quicker and surer because the receiving fielder may have to use the ball immediately to touch a post, or to put it in the square to end an innings.

# Underarm throwing

The throw is most useful for short distances. The ball is thrown from below the level of the shoulders.

## Action

Hold the ball in the throwing hand and swing the arm backwards, close to the body. Right-handed players step forwards with the left foot and *at the same time* swing the right arm forwards and release the ball.

When the ball has been released, the fingers should point in the direction of the throw.

If the ball goes too high, it has been released too late and the fingers will be pointing above the target area. If it is too low, the ball has left the hand too soon and the fingers will be pointing below the target area. (The target area is the receiver's hands.)

When the elementary underarm throw has been mastered, players will find that they can make a more powerful throw if the wrist is 'flicked'.

# Individual fielding places

## Bowler

It is often forgotten that the bowler is still an important member of the fielding team after he has bowled. He may, for example, stop a hit and pass the ball quickly to first post. His greatest value is that when he has the ball in his square, no batter may pass or leave a post. Consider fig. 25.

The batter hits the ball and runs to second post. The ball is returned to the bowler. Let us suppose that the batter at third post loses contact with the post. A throw to fourth post would result in his being put out. On the other hand, a bad throw to fourth post or a careless return to the bowler might result in the batter at second post getting home and scoring. Perhaps it is wiser for the bowler always to keep the ball unless the batter who hit it has been put out or prevented from scoring.

Teams which field with an outside semi-circle of six fielders sometimes use the bowler to receive a poor throw from the first deep fielder after a hit in that direction.

Do not bowl until all of your fielders are in position, ready to field the ball.

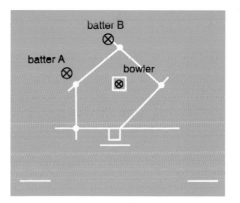

▲ *Fig. 25  Batter B is the 'live' batter, but he cannot run on and score a rounder if the bowler has possession of the ball in the bowling square*

# Backstop

The player acting as backstop must be agile and untiring. He should practise standing as close to the batter as possible (behind the backstop line and without impeding the batter's hitting action), in order to catch the ball before it bounces. He should choose the stance from which he moves fastest and should field behind the bat, not behind the batter, and always be careful not to be unsighted by the batter.

The backstop nearly always throws to first post, but this is not essential. If the batter in the square is weak and there is a good batter running to third post.

The backstop should move according to the bowler's action and should practise with all his bowlers to get used to their different actions.

Backstops should be accurate in their throwing. The ball must always be thrown on the inside of the posts; otherwise, the fielder may be forced to obstruct the batter.

Backstops often drop the ball because they are anxious about throwing the ball to get a batter out at a post. The watchwords are CATCH–THROW, concentrating on each skill separately.

Some teams use the backstop as a fourth post fielder, or as a cover for fielder at fourth post.

# Post play

A post fielder, like all other fielders, should have his weight evenly balanced with feet slightly apart, ready to move quickly in any direction. He should be on the inside and close to the post so that he can touch it quickly without turning.

Where a team choooses to have players at each of the posts in an inner semi-circle, the low balls and short catches are picked up by the post fielders.

A batter can only be put out at a post if he is moving towards it when it is touched with the ball or the hand holding the ball.

If the 'live' batter stops at a post and a fielder touches the post immediately ahead of the batter, he will be prevented from scoring should he run on.

It is possible, with quick teamwork, to catch out one batter, touch out a second, and throw the ball to another post fielder to touch out a third.

# First post fielder

Good 'give' in the hands and arms is necessary as balls are often thrown swiftly from the backstop. A left-handed player is useful here; his left hand is near the post and he is able to touch it without moving. The fielder should practise accurate throwing to third and fourth posts so that he is able to get out a second batter with the same ball.

The first post fielder should back up the bowler when balls come to him from the deep field beyond third and fourth posts. He should also back up in the batting square when there is likely to be a put out in the square at the end of an innings and the backstop is backing up at fourth post. When a left-handed player is batting, the first post fielder must be ready to field oblique hits on the right of the batting square, including mis-hits into the backward area.

The first post fielder normally goes into the deep field for the last batter. He is no longer needed at his post as the ball may be put out in the batting square.

All teams field with a first post fielder, except in special circumstances as described above, as the batter is often put out at first post after missing the ball.

Although it is not compulsory to have fielders standing by the other posts, some teams like to arrange their fielders in this way.

# Second post fielder

The second post fielder is more of a deep than a post fielder and should be capable of covering a wide area, in co-operation with the bowler who will take his place in emergencies. He often has to work 'blind' as the bowler's action may obstruct his view of the batter's bat.

# Third post fielder

The third post fielder should be an experienced player because this is probably the most important post position. He frequently receives catches and many low-driven ground balls. He must take care not to obstruct running batters when a ball is driven wide of the post, or when taking inaccurate throws from the deep or from first post. It is better to take a ball late, after the batter has passed the post, and then neatly flick it to fourth post, than to obstruct a batter and thus give away a half rounder *and* not put him out.

# Fourth post fielder

The fourth post fielder needs safe hands for widely differing types of ball:

• long throws from the deep
• short hits and catches from the batter
• quick passes from third post
• frequent throws from first post, to put out a second batter after one has been put out at first post.

# Deep fielders

Deep fielders must be swift, able to catch any kind of ball and anticipate the direction of the ground balls. They should be ready to cover each other. The first deep fielder should be ready to cover first post for bad throws from the backstop.

Deep fielders should listen for the call from the fielders in the inner circle so that they know where to throw the ball.

Long and accurate throwing is a skill which needs to be practised by the deep fielders. Throw the ball so that the fielders on the posts do not obstruct the batter running round the track.

Deep fielders should be ready to change positions; listening for instructions from the backstop.

*Note* Details of the NRA Coaching Awards can be obtained from the NRA Coaching Secretary at the address given on page 3.

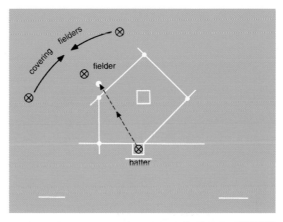

◀ *Fig. 26  Fielders should always be ready to cover each other*

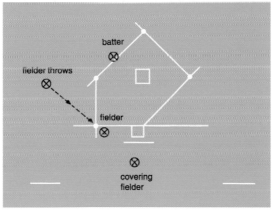

◀ *Fig. 27  Covering a throw*

# A good team

We have discussed the various aspects of the game of rounders, the skills of bowling, batting and fielding. In matches between two teams equally competent in these techniques, one side will be far more successful. Why? What makes a good team?

## Teamwork

First of all, they are a team and not nine individuals. They work together and help each other throughout the game. They enjoy playing rounders.

## Tactics

They know the rules. They think about the game and play intelligently. For example, if they bat first and make a low score, they will probably set a defensive field. It is important to prevent the opposing team from scoring, as well as to get them out. It is a field chosen for a specific set of circumstances. The bowler will be extra careful to avoid offering balls that can be hit easily into the vulnerable area behind the first post. He may achieve this by bowling mainly from the right-hand side of the square, diagonally across the batter.

Another example – when only two batters remain, one rather stronger than the other, the team may decide to avoid putting out the weaker of the pair. If the weaker batter can only reach first post when he bats, there is a good chance of putting both batters out by placing the ball in the batting square. The more dangerous batter is thus prevented from receiving 'the best of three'.

When batting, the players will run as far round the track as possible, moving on at every opportunity until the bowler has the ball They will realise that in the event of any overthrow or misfield it is far better to be already at third post than to be waiting at second. They will turn fielding lapses into rounders by putting pressure on the post fielders.

## The best result

A good team then, consists of members who play rounders rather than play at rounders. They may not, probably will not, always win. They will, however, achieve their best possible result by using fully their abilities and by making the most of the opportunities arising during the game.

## Conclusion

All rounders teams bat, bowl and field. Make sure your team is one that bats, bowls, fields and thinks.

# Captains

Captains should take responsibility for the team and should know the rules. A captain's duties include the following:

- toss for choice of innings
- decide the batting order and, if necessary, change it for the second innings. The umpires must be notified when any change is made
- if there are scorers, the captain must see that they have the batting order and are notified of any changes for the second innings
- if his team uses arm bands or numbers, he should see they are worn
- arrange his field with his bowlers
- change his bowlers correctly. The procedure is as follows: when the ball is in the bowler's hands in the square, he should signal to the umpires to give him a pause, make his arrangements, and say when he has completed the changes

- examine the pitch before a match begins. Apart from clear and correct measurements, there should be a solid line defining the forward and backward area
- make a substitution, if required, in a dead ball situation. The two umpires and the other team must be informed of this change
- remember to thank the umpires and scorers at the end of the match.

# Umpires

Players who are keen to understand the game should try umpiring. There are two umpires, the batter's umpire and the bowler's umpire.

Though the umpires' duties are divided, they must both concentrate on the game at all times and consult each other over difficult points. One umpire may be unsighted and the other may be able to help him to give a decision. Decisions should be called loudly so that they can be heard by all the players.

Both umpires must watch to see that batters do not start to run during the bowler's action before he releases the ball. For infringements of this rule by the batting side, the umpire declares the defaulter(s) out.

## Batter's umpire

The batter's umpire stands where he can see the batter and the first post, *without having to turn his head*. This means as far back as possible, remembering that he also has to be able to see the front lines of both squares. Badly marked squares or unmown grass areas necessitate his standing nearer than is comfortable.

- He watches the ball as it passes the batter, and if it is above or below the limits described on page 22 he calls 'No-ball'.
- Donkey-drops must be watched carefully. When they are travelling between the bowler and the batter they may be any height, but they must pass the batter at the correct height, otherwise, they are no-balls. 'No-ball' must be called loudly enough for all players to hear. *Note* The height of the ball is judged in relation to the batter's height.

- He must also watch the play at first and fourth posts. If either of these posts is touched as a batter is running towards it, he must call 'Out'.
- He must watch for catches and call 'Out' if the ball is held. No part of the ball must touch the ground. He must watch in case the ball is thrown on to another fielder to try to put out a second batter with the same ball.
- He must call 'Rounder' when a batter touches fourth post, having completed the circuit before the next ball is bowled. He must call 'No score' if a batter completes his circuit having run on after a 'live' post has been touched by a fielder.
- He must call 'Half rounder' when a circuit is completed by a batter who did not hit the ball.
- If the ball drops into the backward area, the umpire's call is 'Backward hit'.
- He must watch the front line of the bowling square in case the bowler

steps over it before the ball leaves his hand. He is allowed to step out after the ball has left his hand.

• He must watch the bowler's wrist action. The bowler may not jerk the ball, but must deliver it smoothly.

• He must watch the front and back lines of the batting square. If the batter, in hitting the ball, steps over these lines, he is out.

• If a batter, when off course, obstructs a fielder, he is given out. If a fielder obstructs, the batter is awarded a half rounder. Obstruction may occur (a) when a deep fielder runs into the post area to take a catch between the posts; (b) when a post fielder tries to put out a batter and gets in his way. If batter and fielder are equally guilty of obstruction, they should both be warned.

## Bowler's umpire

• He calls 'Play' to begin the game. If a team is slow to begin again after a no-ball has been bowled, or when there is a bowling change, he calls 'Play' again.

• He calls 'No-ball' if the ball passes the batter on either side of the imaginary rectangle shown on page 22. As the ball may swerve in and out, a no-ball should not be called before the ball reaches the batter. It is the batter's fault, if he moves into, or draws away from, the line of the ball.

• He gives decisions at second and third posts for in/out, obstructions, or when a batter runs inside the posts.

• He calls 'No-ball' if the bowler puts his foot over the back or side lines of the square during his bowling action. Since bowlers' actions differ, the umpire must move about to keep a clear view of the ball.

## Umpire's test

Details of the umpire's test can be obtained from the NRA Umpire's Secretary at the address given on page 3.

▶ *Fig. 29 Umpires work as a team.*
*Be ready to move to a better position. Consult but do not publicly overrule each other's decision.*

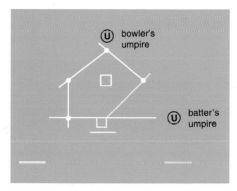

▲ *Fig. 28 Suggested position of umpires. If only one umpire is available, the umpire should adjudicate from the bowler's umpire position.*

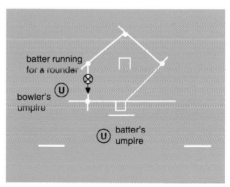

# Scoring

The simplest way of keeping score is for both umpires to have a piece of paper and a pencil. On the paper keep a tally of the rounders and half rounders as they are scored, and keep a record of the number of players out.

## Score sheet

A more detailed record can be kept on a batting score sheet, *see* fig. 30.

- If the batter does not score, put a dot in the appropriate square.
- If the batter scores a rounder, put 1.
- If the batter scores a half rounder (including, an obstruction penalty), put ½.
- If the batter is out, put x.
- If a no-ball is bowled, put a letter N in the square so that you can keep a record of the no-balls. Two consecutive no-balls to the same batter means a half rounder is awarded.

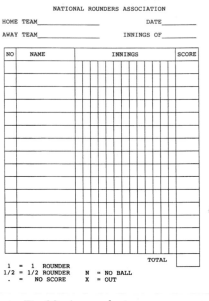

NATIONAL ROUNDERS ASSOCIATION

HOME TEAM_____  DATE_____

AWAY TEAM_____  INNINGS OF_____

| NO | NAME | INNINGS | SCORE |
|----|------|---------|-------|
|    |      |         |       |

| 1 = 1 ROUNDER | | |
| 1/2 = 1/2 ROUNDER | N = NO BALL |
| . = NO SCORE | X = OUT |

TOTAL

▲ *Fig. 30  A score sheet*

# Variations

Rounders is a game which is accessible to all people, including those with special needs and disabilities.

The game of rounders can be adapted to meet the needs of everyone's ability.

When considering adapting rounders, it is important to adhere to the spirit of the game.

## Equipment changes – a check list

- Use larger/smaller balls – foam, air flow, ball with 'bell', bean-bag ball, etc.
- Use lower or lighter equipment – cones, plastic bats, padder bats, paddle bats, etc.
- Use brightly coloured equipment.
- Use batting Ts, e.g. a cone with a ball on the top, for those who have difficulty hitting moving balls.
- Reduce the playing area, e.g. use three posts instead of four.

# T-ball rounders

- Minimum number of players; four per team.
- Batting team: four batters.
- Fielding team: three deep fielders; one player to cover the posts had to put the ball on the T-stand.
- Equipment: one T-stand or large cone; one suitable ball; four bats (one for reach player); four cones as posts.
- Rules: NRA rules, except for the following.
(1) The ball is placed on the T-stand for the batter to hit.
(2) The batter scores one point for reaching first post (before the ball is called dead), two points for second, three points for third, six points for a rounder.
(3) A team is out when four batters are out, but when individuals are out they can rejoin the waiting line and they can bat again and be out again. A team is out when four are out in total.
(4) The dead ball rule. Batters can continue to run until the ball is dead. The ball is dead from when the post ahead of the 'live' batter is touched until the next batter hits the ball of the T-stand.

# Adaptation

T-ball rounders can be used and adapted for all those who have difficulty in hitting a moving ball.

Rule changes may need to be made to suit the ability of the group or individuals. Whatever the changes, though, the name of the game is rounders.

Other variations can be found in the NRA publication Rounders Practices. Details of all NRA publications can be obtained from the NRA Publications Secretary at the address on page 3.

# Index